MIRROR REFLECTIONS

ENCOURAGING GIRLS TO SPEAK ABOUT HIDDEN EMOTIONS

FROM THE PEN OF

Edited by:
Book Formatting: Write on Promotions
Cover by: Photograph by:
Printed and manufactured in the United States of America.
ISBN: 9798877581753
Registered with the Library of Congress.

Mirror Reflections

Encouraging Girls to Speak About Hidden Emotions

TABLE OF CONTENTS

Mirror Reflections

This book is dedicated to all the pretty girls out there who think they are the only ones with hidden emotions. I hope that once you have completed this workbook, you will find out that you are not alone.

HI PRETTY GIRL

Welcome to this transformative journaling journey, where we delve into the intricate landscape of teenage emotions and the profound impact of acknowledging hidden feelings. Adolescence is a time of rapid change, self-discovery, and emotional turbulence. Amid the complexities of growing up, many you grapple with emotions that often go unnoticed or unexpressed.

The pages of this journal are a safe space for self-reflection and exploration, inspired by the powerful metaphor of the mirror. Mirrors reflect not only our physical appearance but also serve as a gateway to our inner selves. you are a metaphorical lens through which we can uncover hidden emotions and navigate the depths of our feelings.

Why Address Hidden Emotions?
Understanding and addressing hidden emotions is crucial for the holistic well-being of you. Unexpressed feelings can manifest in various ways, affecting mental health, relationships, and overall life satisfaction. By acknowledging and dealing with these emotions, we empower ourselves to build resilience, nurture positive mental health, and cultivate meaningful connections with others.

The Mirror Metaphor: A Tool for Insight
Imagine standing in front of a mirror, not merely to see your external reflection but to peer into the recesses of your emotions. This journal invites you to embrace the mirror metaphor as a tool for self-reflection and understanding. The mirror symbolizes a space where authenticity reigns, allowing you to confront and explore the emotions that may be concealed beneath the surface.

Much like a mirror reveals both light and shadow, this metaphor encourages you to acknowledge the full spectrum of your feelings. Through guided exercises and thoughtful prompts, you will embark on a journey of self-discovery, using the mirror as a catalyst for personal growth and emotional intelligence.

As you turn the pages, remember that this journal is a companion on your quest to unravel hidden emotions, fostering a deeper connection with yourself. May the mirror metaphor guide you towards a profound understanding of your feelings and pave the way for open communication, self-acceptance, and a richer, more fulfilling life.

Sincerely,

Dr. Ni'cola

Chapter 1

Understanding Hidden Emotions

Introduction:

Inderstanding our emotions is a crucial step towards maintaining mental well-being. Often, emotions are omplex, and some may be hidden beneath the surface. In this journal entry, we will delve into the concept of idden emotions and explore what it means to identify and acknowledge you.

I
CONTROL
ME.

Define Hidden Emotions:
Take a moment to reflect on what the term "hidden emotions" means to you. How would you describe emotions that are not readily apparent to others or even to yourself?

Consider instances in your life when you may have experienced emotions that you didn't express outwardly or were not fully aware of at the time.

Personal Experiences:
Share a specific situation where you felt emotions were hidden or not easily recognizable. What were those emotions, and why do you think you remained concealed?

Reflect on the impact of keeping these emotions hidden. Did it affect your well-being, relationships, or overall mindset?

Cultural and Social Influences:
Explore how cultural or societal expectations might contribute to the hiding of emotions. Are there societal norms that discourage expressing certain feelings?

Consider any personal experiences where cultural or social expectations influenced how you expressed or concealed your emotions.

The Mask We Wear:

Think about the concept of wearing a "mask" to hide your true emotions from others. What does this mask look like, and why might you wear it?

Reflect on the challenges and benefits of removing this emotional mask. What fears or concerns might arise, and what positive outcomes could result from being more authentic?

Desired Emotional Expression:

Envision a scenario where you feel comfortable expressing all your emotions openly. What does that look like? How would it impact your relationships and your overall well-being?

Consider steps you can take to create an environment that encourages open and honest emotional expression.

Conclusion:

Reflect on what you have learned about hidden emotions through this journal entry. Consider any insights gained and whether there are aspects of your emotional life that you'd like to explore further or share with others.

Remember, this journal is a personal space for self-reflection, and there are no right or wrong answers. Feel free to express your thoughts openly and honestly.

WHY DO GIRLS HIDE YOUR FEELINGS?

REAL-LIFE EXAMPLES TO ILLUSTRATE HIDDEN EMOTIONS

Academic Pressure:: A high-achieving teen girl might consistently excel in academics but secretly struggle with immense pressure to maintain her performance. Hidden emotions may include fear of failure, anxiety about meeting expectations, and self-doubt despite outward success.

Social Media Comparison: A teenage girl may project confidence on social med platforms, showcasing a seemingly perfect life. However, behind the carefully curated posts, she may be dealing with feelings of inadequacy, comparison, an the pressure to conform to societal standards of beauty and success.

Bullying and Harassment: A teen girl who is a target of bullying may conceal feelings of fear, shame, and isolation. She might project strength but harbor hidc emotions related to the psychological toll of being mistreated.

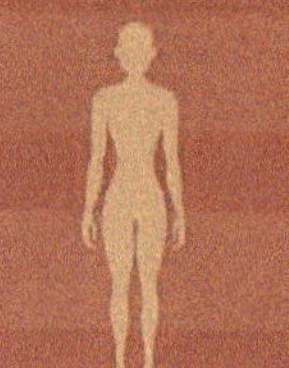

Body Image Issues: A teen girl may go to great lengths to hide struggles with body image. Despite appearing confident, she may battle with self-esteem issu negative self-talk, and the pressure to meet unrealistic beauty standards.

Family Expectations: A girl from a traditional family may hide feelings of conflic between her aspirations and the expectations placed on her by family members This can lead to a struggle with identity and a fear of disappointing loved ones.

Friendship Dynamics: A teen girl who appears to have a strong group of friends may be concealing feelings of loneliness, exclusion, or insecurity within the group. Hidden emotions may include a fear of rejection and the pressure to conform to peer expectations.

Romantic Relationships: A girl in a seemingly perfect romantic relationship may concealing emotions related to insecurity, fear of vulnerability, or concerns abou the future. Hidden emotions may manifest in the form of jealousy, possessivenes or a fear of being truly known.

Sexual Identity Exploration: A teen girl exploring her sexual identity may hide feelings of confusion, fear of judgment, or the struggle to come to terms with h identity. Concealing these emotions may be a coping mechanism in an environment where acceptance is uncertain.

Explore the concept of hidden emotions and why you might suppress or hide your feelings.

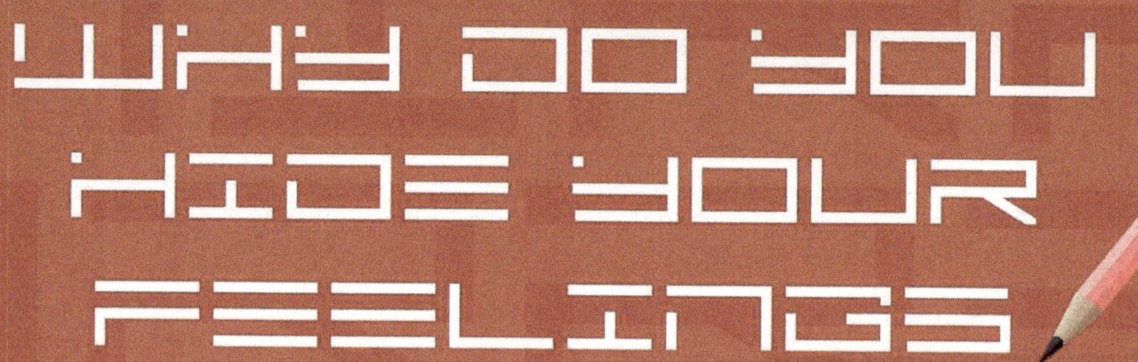

Explore the concept of hidden emotions and why you might suppress or hide your feelings

Explore the concept of hidden emotions and why you might suppress or hide your feelings.

Explore the concept of hidden emotions and why you might suppress or hide your feelings

HEALTHY TIPS

After completing this section, answer the following questions.

ESSENTIAL QUESTION

How can you develop your mindset to set yourself up for growth?

Chapter 2

The Mirror Metaphor

THE MIRROR METAPHOR

Introduction:

In the journey of self-discovery and emotional well-being, the mirror metaphor serves as a powerful and enlightening tool. Much like a physical mirror reflects our external appearance, the mirror metaphor is designed to reflect our internal landscape—the often hidden realm of our emotions. By understanding and embracing this metaphor, you can embark on a ransformative process of self-reflection, unlocking the otential to explore and express your hidden emotions.

How the Mirror Metaphor Works:

The mirror metaphor invites you to engage in a guided visualizatio exercise. You are encouraged to visualize standing in front of thi emotional mirror, observing your reflections, and gradually peelin back the layers to reveal the emotions that may be concealed. Thi process facilitates a connection with one's inner self, promotin self-discovery and encouraging an open dialogue with one' emotions.

As we embark on this journey together, let the mirror metaphor be guiding light, illuminating the path toward a deeper understandin of hidden emotions. Through self-reflection and embracing th mirror within, you can cultivate a healthier relationship with you emotions, fostering personal growth and emotional well-being.

Understanding the Mirror Metaphor:

Imagine standing in front of a mirror, observing not just your external features, but delving deeper to see your emotions, thoughts, and innermost feelings. The mirror metaphor encourages you to look within yourself, exploring the complexities of your emotions that might be concealed beneath the surface. It acts as a symbolic gateway to self-awareness and personal growth.

Visual Representation:

To enhance the grasp of the mirror metaphor, consider it as a mental and emotional mirror that reflects the unseen aspects of oneself. Picture a mirror that not only reveals the immediate emotions on the surface but also can unveil the more subtle, hidden feelings that might be tucked away in the corners of the mind. This visual representation is a reminder that our emotions are multifaceted, and just like a mirror, you can be uncovered and acknowledged.

”
I LOVE ME!

Guided Visualization Exercise: Exploring Hidden Emotions with the Mirror Metaphor

Begin by finding a quiet and comfortable space. Sit or lie down in a relaxed position. Take a few deep breaths to center yourself.

Step 1: Creating a Safe Space

Close your eyes and visualize a peaceful and safe space. It could b a quiet room, a beautiful garden, or a serene beach. Imagine th details – the colors, sounds, and smells of this calming environment Feel a sense of safety and comfort as you enter this space.

Step 2: The Mirror Appears

In the center of this safe space, visualize a mirror. This mirror is no an ordinary one; it's a magical mirror that reflects your inne emotions and thoughts. Imagine it appearing before you, reflectin only what you are ready to see.

Step 3: Gazing into the Mirror

Approach the mirror with curiosity. As you look into it, notice you reflection. Take a moment to observe your facial expressions, bod language, and the energy surrounding you in the reflection. Th mirror is a gateway to your hidden emotions.

Step 4: Exploring Hidden Emotions

Now, imagine that the mirror starts to reveal images, symbols, o colors that represent your hidden emotions. It might show scene from your past, present, or even your future. Allow these images t surface without judgment. Take your time to explore an understand what each representation means to you.

Step 5: Engaging with the Emotions

As you observe these reflections, acknowledge the emotions that come up. It could be joy, sadness, fear, or a mix of feelings. Allow yourself to experience these emotions fully. Remember, this is a safe space, and you have control over the process.

Step 6: Expressing Emotions

If you feel comfortable, express your emotions in this space. You can speak to your reflection, write down your thoughts, or simply let the emotions flow. The mirror is a non-judgmental space where you can be honest with yourself.

Step 7: Embracing Acceptance

As you engage with your hidden emotions, visualize a sense of acceptance and self-compassion enveloping you. Imagine the mirror transforming into a source of empowerment, where you can face and overcome challenges with newfound strength.

Step 8: Closing the Visualization

Gently bring your awareness back to the present moment. Take a few deep breaths, slowly opening your eyes when you're ready. Reflect on the experience, and consider jotting down any insights or emotions that arose during the exercise.

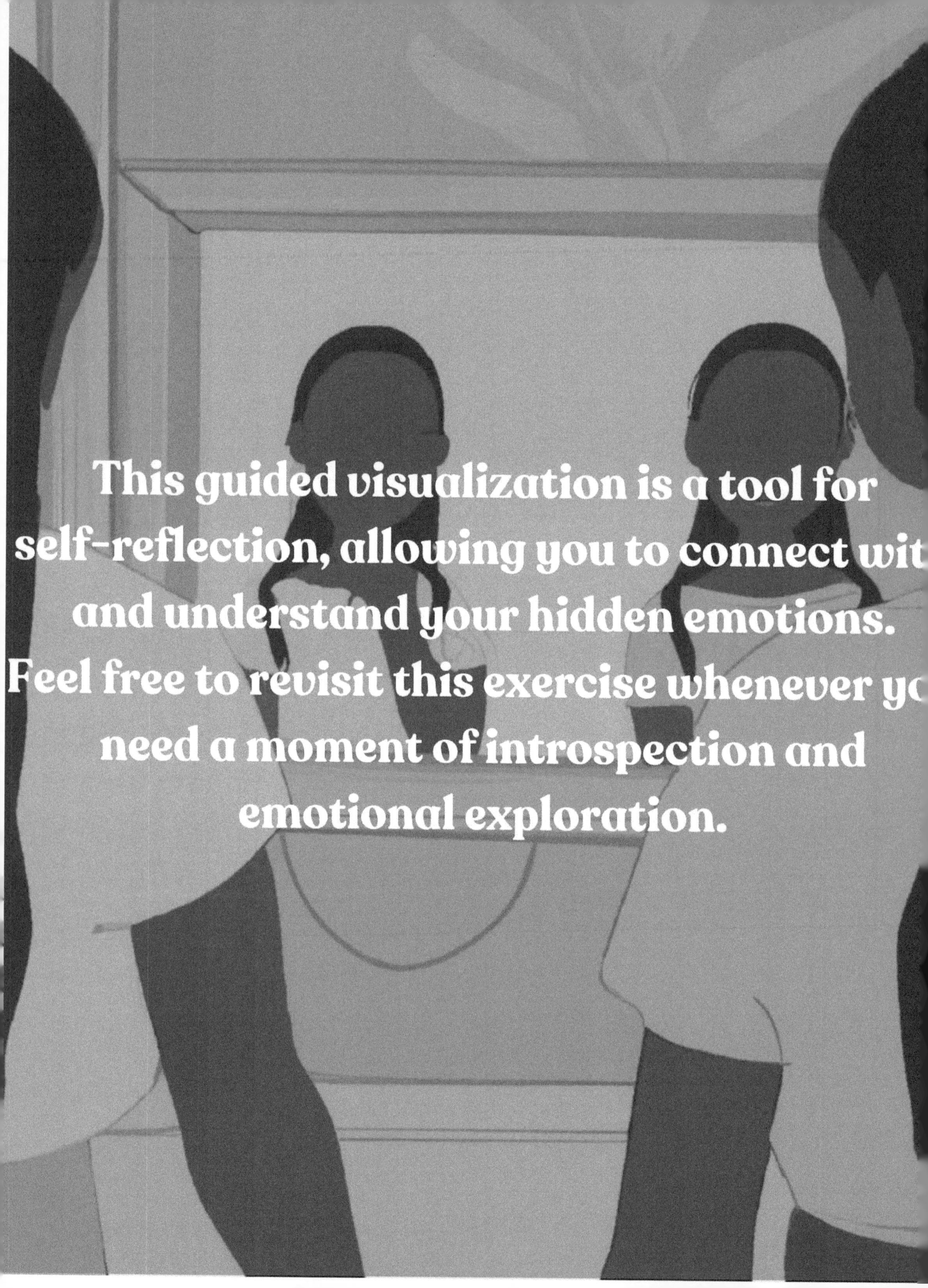

This guided visualization is a tool for self-reflection, allowing you to connect wit and understand your hidden emotions. Feel free to revisit this exercise whenever yo need a moment of introspection and emotional exploration.

HEALTHY

TIPS

After completing this section, answer the following questions.

ESSENTIAL QUESTION

How can you develop your mindset to set yourself up for growth?

Chapter 3

Identifying and Expressing Emotions

FEARLESS

ffective communication is the cornerstone of healthy relationships, fostering understanding, trust, and emotional well-being. In the context of addressing hidden motions, open communication becomes even more critical. This article underscores the significance of transparent communication nd provides tips for both teenagers and those supporting them.

Building Trust:

Open communication is essential for building trust in any relationship. When individuals feel comfortable expressing their thoughts and emotions without fear of judgment, trust is nurtured. This trust forms a solid foundation for addressing hidden emotions as individuals are more likely to reveal their true feelings.

Fostering Understanding:

Hidden emotions often stem from a lack of understanding or miscommunication. Encouraging open dialogue helps to clarify misunderstandings and provides an opportunity for you to express yourself authentically. This fosters a deeper understanding of each other's perspectives and feelings.

Emotional Well-being:

Suppressing emotions can have detrimental effects on mental health. Open communication provides an outlet for you to share your feelings, reducing the burden on your emotional well-being. It allows for the acknowledgment and validation of emotions promoting a healthier mental state.

Creating a Supportive Environment:

You, in particular, may hesitate to share your emotions due to fear of judgment or criticism. Establishing a supportive environment through open communication reassures them that your feelings are valid and creates a space where they feel comfortable seeking guidance or sharing your concerns.

Active Listening:
Effective communication involves not only expressing oneself but also actively listening to others. Encouraging you and those supporting you to practice active listening—paying full attention, avoiding interruptions, and empathizing with the speaker. This fosters a two-way street of communication.

Encouraging Expression:
You may find it challenging to articulate your emotions. I encourage the use of various forms of expression, such as journaling, art, or music, to help you communicate your feelings. This allows for a more nuanced understanding of your emotions.

Promoting Patience:
Addressing hidden emotions requires patience. Remember that it's okay to take the time you need to process your feelings. Encourage a patient and non-judgmental approach to communication, allowing emotions to unfold naturally.

In conclusion, open communication is the key to unveiling hidden emotions and promoting emotional well-being. By building trust, fostering understanding, and creating a supportive environment, you can navigate your emotions more effectively. Tips such as active listening, encouraging expression, and promoting patience further enhance the effectiveness of communication, particularly for teenagers. Embracing open communication is a powerful tool for building stronger connections and ensuring the emotional health of individuals and relationships alike.

MIRROR MIRROR ON THE WALL...

Exercise 1

Objective:

To foster self-awareness by encouraging you to reflect on your daily emotions.

Instructions:

- Use the following journal pages to record your emotions every day.
- Journal about your emotions at different points in the day.
- Describe the events or situations that triggered specific emotions.
- By the end of the week, reflect on the patterns and changes in your emotional experiences.

DAY 1

DAY 1

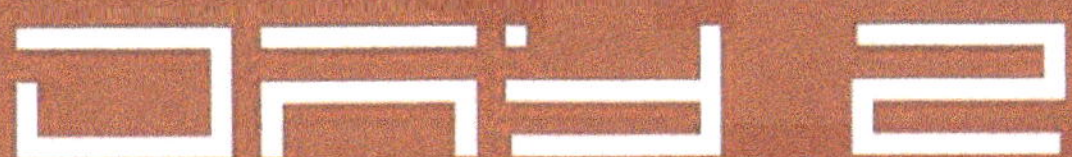
DAY 2

DAY 2

DAY 3

DAY 3

DAY 4

DAY 4

DAY 5

DAY 5

DAY 6

DAY 6

DAY 7

Exercise 2

Emotion Wheel

Objective:

To visually represent and categorize a wide range of emotions.

Instructions:

- Use the emotion wheel below to fill in different sections with emotions that you commonly experience.
- Journal the complexity and interconnectedness of emotions on the wheel.
- Once complete, explore the variety of emotions identified on the wheel.
- Think about the idea that emotions are nuanced and interconnected.
- Think about the importance of recognizing and accepting the full spectrum of emotions.

EMOTION
WHEEL

EMOTION
WHEEL

EMOTION
WHEEL

EMOTION
WHEEL

EMOTION
WHEEL

EMOTION
WHEEL

EMOTION
WHEEL

WHAT ARE YOUR
THOUGHTS ON
YOUR
EMOTIONAL
PATTERN?

WHAT ARE YOUR THOUGHTS ON YOUR EMOTIONAL PATTERN?

WHAT ARE YOUR
THOUGHTS ON
YOUR
EMOTIONAL
PATTERN?

WHAT ARE YOUR THOUGHTS ON YOUR EMOTIONAL PATTERN?

WHAT ARE YOUR
THOUGHTS ON
YOUR
EMOTIONAL
PATTERN?

WHAT ARE YOUR
THOUGHTS ON
YOUR
EMOTIONAL
PATTERN?

WHAT ARE YOUR THOUGHTS ON YOUR EMOTIONAL PATTERN?

HEALTHY
TIPS

After completing this section, answer the following questions.

ESSENTIAL QUESTION

What are some ways that you can you control your emotions on your own?

In the bustling realm of teenage emotions, navigating the turbulent waters of self-expression becomes crucial for personal growth and mental well-being. "Emotional Canvas" is a project designed to harness the therapeutic power of artistic expression among girls. Through diverse creative activities such as drawing and writing this initiative aims to provide a safe space for adolescents to explore, communicate, and ultimately understand your emotions.

I AM
CREATIVE.

I AM BEAUTIFUL

Exercise 1

Drawing Emotions

Artistic expression through drawing is a powerful medium for girls to visually communicate your feelings.

Use the sections below to create visual representations of your emotions, whether through abstract art or sketching.

The act of drawing serves as a cathartic release, allowing you to externalize and reflect upon your internal struggles.

DRAW YOUR

DAY 1

DAY 2

DAY 3

DAY 4

DRAW YOUR

DAY 5

DAY 6

DAY 7

Exercise 2

Penning Personal Narratives

Writing offers a unique avenue for introspection and self-discovery.

Use the sections below to journal your thoughts, feelings, and experiences, fostering a deeper understanding of your emotional landscapes.

Narrative therapy exercises and prompts will empower you to transform your emotions into written form, providing an outlet for self-expression and a tool for emotional resilience.

THOUGHTS
JOURNAL

THOUGHTS JOURNAL

THOUGHTS
JOURNAL

THOUGHTS
JOURNAL

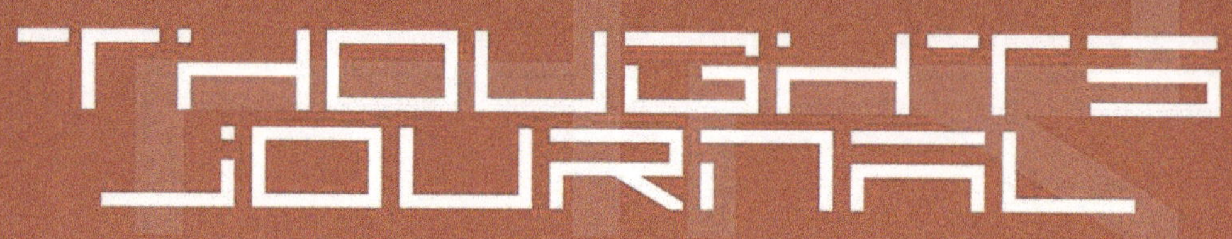
THOUGHTS
JOURNAL

THOUGHTS
JOURNAL

"Emotional Canvas" strives to be more than a creative outlet; it is a journey of self-discovery and healing for you to navigate the complexities of adolescence.

By embracing drawing, writing, and music as mediums of expression, this project aims to showcase the profound therapeutic benefits of artistic engagement, empowering you to embrace your emotions and embark on a path of holistic well-being.

HEALTHY
TIPS

After completing this section, answer the following questions.

ESSENTIAL QUESTION

Do you think that using artistic tools can really help you channel your emotions?

Chapter 4

Building a Support System

BUILDING A SUPPORT SYSTEM

Effective communication is the cornerstone of healthy relationships, fostering understanding, trust, and emotional well-being. In the context of addressing hidden emotions, open communication becomes even more critical. This section underscores the significance of transparent communication and provides tips for both you and your loved ones.

WHAT ABOUT YOUR FRIENDS

Building Trust:

Open communication is essential for building trust in any relationship. When individuals feel comfortable expressing your thoughts and emotions without fear of judgment, trust is nurtured. This trust forms a solid foundation for addressing hidden emotions as individuals are more likely to reveal your true feelings.

Fostering Understanding:

Hidden emotions often stem from a lack of understanding or miscommunication. Encouraging open dialogue helps to clarify misunderstandings and provides an opportunity for individuals to express youselves authentically. This fosters a deeper understanding of each other's perspectives and feelings.

Emotional Well-being:

Suppressing emotions can have detrimental effects on mental health. Open communication provides an outlet for you to share your feelings, reducing the burden on your emotional well-being. It allows for the acknowledgment and validation of emotions, promoting a healthier mental state.

Creating a Supportive Environment:

You, in particular, may hesitate to share your emotions due to fear of judgment or criticism. Establishing a supportive environment through open communication reassures you that your feelings are valid and creates a space where you feel comfortable seeking guidance or sharing your concerns.

Active Listening:
Effective communication involves not only expressing oneself but also actively listening to others. Encourage you and those supporting you to practice active listening—paying full attention, avoiding interruptions, and empathizing with the speaker. This fosters a two-way street of communication.

Encouraging Expression:
You may find it challenging to articulate your emotions. Encourage the use of various forms of expression, such as journaling, art, or music, to help you communicate your feelings. This allows for a more nuanced understanding of your emotions.

Promoting Patience:
Addressing hidden emotions requires patience. Remember that it's okay to take the time you need to process your feelings. I encourage a patient and non-judgmental approach to communication, allowing emotions to unfold naturally.

In conclusion, open communication is the key to unveiling hidden emotions and promoting emotional well-being. By building trust, fostering understanding, and creating a supportive environment, you can navigate your emotions more effectively. Tips such as active listening, encouraging expression, and promoting patience further enhance the effectiveness of communication, particularly for you. Embracing open communication is a powerful tool for building stronger connections and ensuring the emotional health of individuals and relationships alike.

Chapter 5

Understanding Hidden Emotions

SEEKING PROFESSIONAL HELP

In today's fast-paced world, you will face a myriad of challenges that can take a toll on your mental health. Unfortunately, the stigma surrounding mental health often prevents you from seeking the professional help you may desperately need. This journal aims to break down those barriers and encourage a more open dialogue about mental well-being.

The stigma surrounding mental health issues is deeply rooted in misconceptions and stereotypes. you may hesitate to open up about your struggles due to the fear of being labeled as "weak" or "attention-seeking." This stigma can create a barrier, preventing you from seeking the necessary support and guidance.

GETTING HELP IS THE NEW FLEX

DESTIGMATIZING MENTAL HEALTH:

Normalize the Conversation:
Begin by normalizing discussions around mental health at home, in schools, and within the community. By making it a regular topic of conversation, you are more likely to feel comfortable discussing your own experiences.

Educate on Mental Health:
Lack of understanding contributes to stigma. Providing accurate information about mental health conditions and treatment options helps dispel myths and promotes empathy. Schools can incorporate mental health education into your curriculum to increase awareness.

Share Personal Stories:
Encourage individuals, including public figures and peers, to share your personal journeys with mental health. Real stories can humanize the experience, making it easier for you to relate and understand that seeking help is a sign of strength.

STRATEGIES FOR BUILDING A SUPPORTIVE NETWORK

This work page is designed to inspire and encourage you on how to lead healthy team-building activities for your friends and family. This will help enhance your supportive network.

Peer Mentoring:

Pair more experienced teens with newcomers to provide guidance and support. This mentorship system creates a sense of belonging and helps build trust among peers.

Regular Check-ins:

Schedule regular check-ins where teens can share their thoughts, experiences, and challenges. This creates a space for open dialogue and allows for mutual support.

Positive Affirmations:

Incorporate positive affirmations and gratitude exercises. Encourage teens to express appreciation for each other, fostering a culture of positivity and support.

Mindfulness & Relaxation Sessions

Introduce mindfulness and relaxation techniques, such as meditation or yoga. These activities can help reduce stress and promote a sense of calm within the group.

10 Resources for help

1. National Suicide Prevention Lifeline
Website: suicidepreventionlifeline.org
Phone: 1-800-273-TALK (1-800-273-8255)

2. Crisis Text Line
Website: crisistextline.org
Text: Text "HOME" to 741741

3. Girls Health.gov - Mental Health Resources
Website: girlshealth.gov/mental-health
Information on mental health topics, resources, and support for girls.

4. The Trevor Project
Website: thetrevorproject.org
TrevorLifeline: 1-866-488-7386
TrevorText: Text "START" to 678678

5. Psychology Today - Find a Therapist
Website: psychologytoday.com
Therapist Directory: Search for therapists by location, specialization, and insurance.

6. 7 Cups
Website: 7cups.com
Online Emotional Support: Connect with trained listeners for free emotional support.

7. RAINN (Rape, Abuse & Incest National Network)
Website: rainn.org
National Sexual Assault Hotline: 1-800-656-HOPE
(1-800-656-4673)

8. National Eating Disorders Association (NEDA) Helpline
Website: nationaleatingdisorders.org
Helpline: 1-800-931-2237

9. Love is Respect
Website: loveisrespect.org
National Dating Abuse Helpline: 1-866-331-9474
Text "LOVEIS" to 22522

10. American Association of Sexuality Educators, Counselors, and Therapists (AASECT)
Website: aasect.org
Directory of Certified Sexuality Educators, Counselors, and Therapists

These resources provide a range of professional assistance, from mental health support to crisis intervention, covering various aspects of well-being for girls. It's crucial to reach out to these organizations for the help and guidance needed during challenging times.

CONCLUSION

In the journey through "Mirror Reflections: Encouraging Tee to Speak About Hidden Emotions," we have delved into th significance of addressing hidden emotions in the lives teenagers. The exploration has underscored the critical role th acknowledging and understanding these emotions plays fostering overall well-being and emotional resilience.

Hidden emotions, often concealed beneath the surface, can exe a profound impact on a teenager's mental health, affecting the relationships, academic performance, and self-esteem. B shedding light on these emotions, we empower teens to confro and navigate the complex landscape of their inner worlds.

Throughout this workbook, we have emphasized the importan of encouraging ongoing self-reflection. The process of lookin within, identifying emotions, and understanding their roots an essential step toward personal growth and emotion intelligence. By fostering a habit of self-awareness, we equi you with the tools needed to navigate life's challenges wit greater resilience and clarity.

HEALTHY

TIPS

After completing this section, answer the following questions.

ESSENTIAL QUESTION

How can you develop your mindset to set yourself up for growth?

CONCLUSION

In the journey through "Mirror Reflections: Encouraging Teen to Speak About Hidden Emotions," we have delved into th significance of addressing hidden emotions in the lives c teenagers. The exploration has underscored the critical role thc acknowledging and understanding these emotions plays i fostering overall well-being and emotional resilience.

Hidden emotions, often concealed beneath the surface, can exe a profound impact on a teenager's mental health, affecting the relationships, academic performance, and self-esteem. B shedding light on these emotions, we empower teens to confror and navigate the complex landscape of their inner worlds.

Throughout this workbook, we have emphasized the importanc of encouraging ongoing self-reflection. The process of lookin within, identifying emotions, and understanding their roots i an essential step toward personal growth and emotionc intelligence. By fostering a habit of self-awareness, we equi you with the tools needed to navigate life's challenges wit greater resilience and clarity.

CONCLUSION

Additionally, we have advocated for seeking support when needed. Adolescence is a transformative period marked by numerous changes, and having a support system is crucial. Whether it be friends, family, or professional counselors, reaching out for help is a sign of strength, not weakness. By dismantling the stigma surrounding seeking support, we hope to create an environment where teens feel comfortable expressing their emotions and seeking assistance when required.

As we conclude our journey through "Mirror Reflections," let us carry forward the understanding that addressing hidden emotions is not only a personal endeavor but a collective responsibility. By fostering open conversations and providing a supportive environment, we contribute to the emotional well-being of the next generation. May this workbook catalyze positive change, inspiring teens to embrace self-reflection, share their hidden emotions, and seek the support they deserve on their path to self-discovery and resilience.

THE "GOOD" IN GOOD-BYE

Dear ______________________,

As I enter this new chapter in my life, entitled ________________ [insert title] , I am reminded of the incredible power of saying goodbye. The last time I had to bid farewell to something was ________________ [insert experience] , and I recall feeling ________________ [insert emotion]. However, I held on to ________________ [insert coping mechanism] to cope with the loss.

I have since learned that every closed door signifies the end of one journey and the beginning of another. Saying goodbye does not mean we should forget the experiences and phases of our lives that have shaped us. In fact, it's a chance to reflect on ________________ [insert reflection] and to embrace new opportunities. As I close the door on ________________ [insert experience] , I am embracing ________________ [insert new experience] with open arms. By doing so, I am creating space for ________________ [insert positive outcomes], ________________ [insert aspirations] , and ________________ [insert goals].

Now, at this pivotal moment, I understand that goodbye is not an end, but a transition - a stepping stone to something greater. I am embracing life's dance and learning to lean into life's transitions. I am excited for what the future holds, and I look forward to ________________ [insert future plans] and everything that God has in store for me.

Here's to taking control of your emotions by looking into the mirror keep going Queens!

Sincerely,

____

Sign heere replacing your middle name with hidden emotions!

MONTHLY PLAN

JAN FEB MAR APR MAY JUN JUL AUG SEP OCT NOV DEC

SUN	MON	TUE	WED	THU	FRI	SAT

NOTES:

MONTHLY GOALS:

TO DO:

MONTHLY AFFIRMATIONS:

MONTHLY PLAN

JAN FEB MAR APR MAY JUN JUL AUG SEP OCT NOV DEC

SUN	MON	TUE	WED	THU	FRI	SAT

NOTES:

MONTHLY GOALS:

TO DO:

MONTHLY AFFIRMATIONS:

MONTHLY PLAN

JAN FEB MAR APR MAY JUN JUL AUG SEP OCT NOV DEC

SUN	MON	TUE	WED	THU	FRI	SAT

NOTES:

MONTHLY GOALS:

TO DO:

MONTHLY AFFIRMATIONS:

MONTHLY PLAN

JAN FEB MAR APR MAY JUN JUL AUG SEP OCT NOV DEC

SUN	MON	TUE	WED	THU	FRI	SAT

NOTES:

MONTHLY GOALS:

TO DO:

MONTHLY AFFIRMATIONS:

MONTHLY PLAN

JAN FEB MAR APR MAY JUN JUL AUG SEP OCT NOV DEC

SUN	MON	TUE	WED	THU	FRI	SAT

NOTES:

MONTHLY GOALS:

TO DO:

MONTHLY AFFIRMATIONS:

MONTHLY PLAN

JAN FEB MAR APR MAY JUN JUL AUG SEP OCT NOV DEC

SUN	MON	TUE	WED	THU	FRI	SAT

NOTES:

MONTHLY GOALS:

TO DO:

MONTHLY AFFIRMATIONS:

MONTHLY PLAN

JAN FEB MAR APR MAY JUN JUL AUG SEP OCT NOV DEC

SUN	MON	TUE	WED	THU	FRI	SAT

NOTES:

MONTHLY GOALS:

TO DO:

MONTHLY AFFIRMATIONS:

MONTHLY PLAN

JAN FEB MAR APR MAY JUN JUL AUG SEP OCT NOV DEC

SUN	MON	TUE	WED	THU	FRI	SAT

NOTES:

MONTHLY GOALS:

TO DO:

MONTHLY AFFIRMATIONS:

NOTES

NOTES

NOTES

NOTES

NOTES

NOTES

Month:

Week Of:

SUNDAY

MONDAY

TUESDAY

WEDNESDAY

THURSDAY

FRIDAY

SATURDAY

NOTES:

Month:

Week Of:

SUNDAY

MONDAY

TUESDAY

WEDNESDAY

THURSDAY

FRIDAY

SATURDAY

NOTES:

Month:

Week Of:

SUNDAY

MONDAY

TUESDAY

WEDNESDAY

THURSDAY

FRIDAY

SATURDAY

Month:

Week Of:

SUNDAY

- [ ]
- [ ]
- [ ]
- [ ]

MONDAY

- [ ]
- [ ]
- [ ]
- [ ]

TUESDAY

- [ ]
- [ ]
- [ ]
- [ ]

WEDNESDAY

- [ ]
- [ ]
- [ ]
- [ ]

THURSDAY

- [ ]
- [ ]
- [ ]
- [ ]

FRIDAY

- [ ]
- [ ]
- [ ]
- [ ]

SATURDAY

- [ ]
- [ ]
- [ ]
- [ ]

NOTES:

Month:

Week Of:

SUNDAY

MONDAY

TUESDAY

WEDNESDAY

THURSDAY

FRIDAY

SATURDAY

NOTES:

Month:

Week Of:

SUNDAY

MONDAY

TUESDAY

WEDNESDAY

THURSDAY

FRIDAY

SATURDAY

NOTES:

Month:

Week Of:

SUNDAY

MONDAY

TUESDAY

WEDNESDAY

THURSDAY

FRIDAY

SATURDAY

Month:

Week Of:

SUNDAY

MONDAY

TUESDAY

WEDNESDAY

THURSDAY

FRIDAY

SATURDAY

NOTES:

hello there

MEET DR. NI'COLA MITCHELL

As an award-winning entrepreneur, Dr. Mitchell has demonstrated her innovative and strategic mindset in various ventures. Notably, she serves as the Executive Producer for Lifetime Movie Network, where she has played a vital role in bringing her compelling story to the screen that captivates audiences and sheds light on important social issues, Giving Hope: the Ni'Cola Mitchell story.

Dr. Ni'Cola Mitchell's impact is undeniable, as evidenced by the tremendous reach of the Girls Who Brunch Tour. Having already touched the lives of over 41,000 girls worldwide, her tireless efforts and dedication have made a tangible difference in the lives of young girls, providing them with the opportunity to achieve their full potential.

Some of her awards are listed below:

- 2024 Intentional Woman Award
- 2023 Spirit of Detroit Award presented by the City Council of Detroit
- 2023 New York State Assembly Citation from Assemblywoman Michaelle Solages
- 2023 Black Authors Festival on Sag Island honoree of the Dr. Ni'Cola Mitchell Lifetime Achievement Award.
- Top 23 of 2023 Winners of the World Global magazine
- Prestigious Congressional recognition from Congresswoman Sheila Jackson Lee
- Proclamation Day: March 26th, 2023 is Ni'Cola Mitchell Day from the City of Houston
- Executive Producer for Lifetime Movie Networks
- The Presidential Lifetime Achievement Award
- Doctorate of Philosophy in Humanitarianism
- Visa She's Next Black Women-Owned Business Grant Recipient
- The People's Uprising Woman of the Year
- Civility for the Girl Child Initiative Honoree
- George H. W. Bush's Daily Points of Light Award
- Forbes List as a Change Maker
- L'Oreal Paris Women of Worth
- Smart Women In Meeting Entrepreneur of the Year
- Women of Distinction Award
- Black Enterprise One of the 5-Follow Worthy Bloggers to Watch
- Several proclamations from the cities of Atlanta, Charleston, Houston, the Mayor's office of Indianapolis, Indiana, the Mayor's office of Las Vegas, Nevada, and New Orleans, LA.

www.ingramcontent.com/pod-product-compliance
Ingram Content Group UK Ltd.
Pitfield, Milton Keynes, MK11 3LW, UK
UKHW062000290726
14090UKWH00021B/1317